INTRODUCTION

Are you new to the world of crocheting, a seasoned professional, or somewhere in-between? No matter what your skill level is, the Crochet Pocket Guide is the perfect resource to add to your crafting toolkit. Compact and easy to take on-the-go, this pocket guide is full of information, tips, and a handy ruler so you can check your gauge! General information about yarn and thread weight and a bank of frequently used abbreviations will help you get started. Detailed instructions and illustrations will guide you through creating a variety of stitches, from a single crochet to clusters, puff stitches, v-stitches, and many more! Additional stitching tips teach you how to join stitches together and change yarn colors mid-project. Grab your pocket guide, some yarn, and your crochet hooks to get started now!

TABLE OF CONTENTS

I0893803

YARN AND THREAD

Yarn and thread are classified by weight, which is determined by the thickness of the strand.

Yarn consists of individual plies twisted together. The number of plies has nothing to do with the weight of the yarn.

Thread sizes range from a thick size 5 to a thin, delicate size 150. The higher the size number, the thinner the thread. The most popular thread size is bedspread weight cotton, size 10.

Fig. 1 shows the actual size of the most commonly used yarn weights, and **Fig. 2** shows the actual size of the most commonly used cotton crochet threads. They can be used as a reference to check the weight of your yarn and thread.

Fig. 1

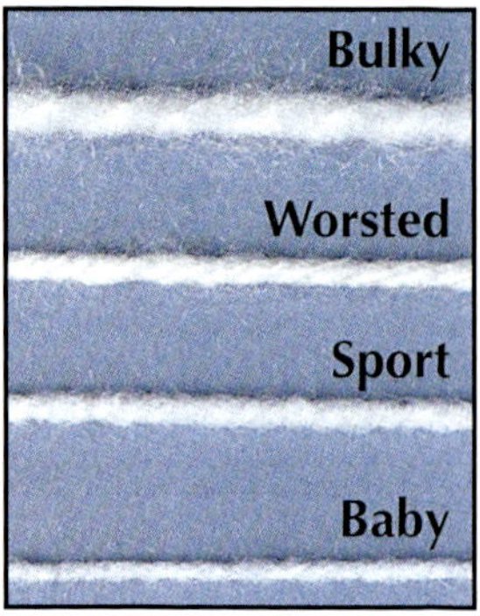

Fig. 2

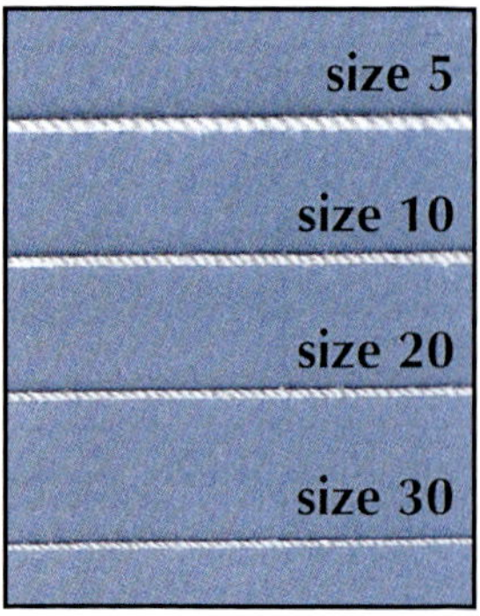

ABBREVIATIONS

The abbreviations most frequently used are listed below. Always refer to the list included in each leaflet.

BPdc	Back Post double crochet(s)
ch	chain(s)
dc	double crochet(s)
dtr	double treble crochet(s)
FPdc	Front Post double crochet(s)
hdc	half double crochet(s)
sc	single crochet(s)
tr	treble crochet(s)
tr tr	triple treble crochet(s)
YO	yarn over

★ — work instructions following ★ as many **more** times as indicated in addition to the first time.

( ) — work enclosed instructions **as many** times as specified by the number immediately following **or** work all enclosed instructions in the stitch or space indicated **or** contains explanatory remarks.

CROCHET STITCHES

SINGLE CROCHET (abbreviated sc)

Insert hook in stitch or space indicated, YO and pull up a loop, YO and draw through both loops on hook **(Fig. 3)**.

Fig. 3

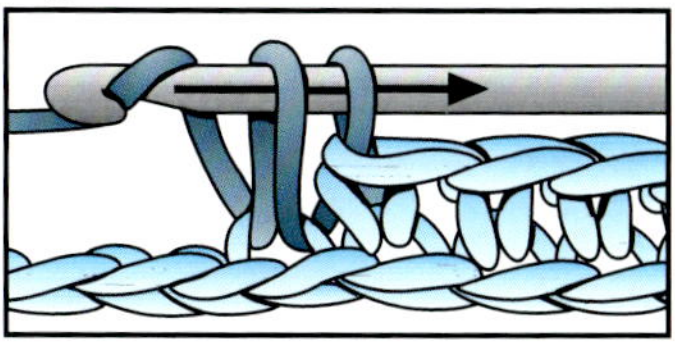

HALF DOUBLE CROCHET (abbreviated hdc)

YO, insert hook in stitch or space indicated, YO and pull up a loop, YO and draw through all 3 loops on hook **(Fig. 4)**.

Fig. 4

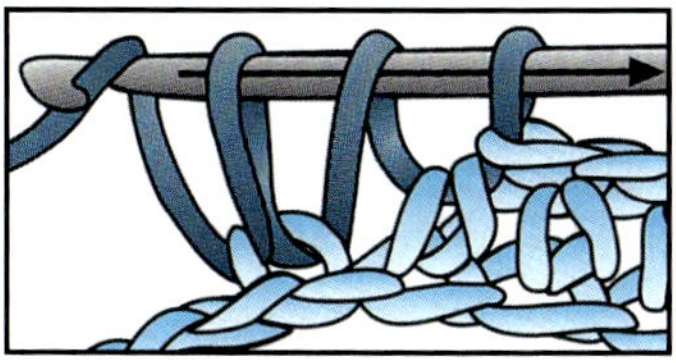

DOUBLE CROCHET (abbreviated dc)

YO, insert hook in stitch or space indicated, YO and pull up a loop (3 loops on hook), YO and draw through 2 loops on hook **(Fig. 5a)**, YO and draw through remaining 2 loops on hook **(Fig. 5b)**.

Fig. 5a

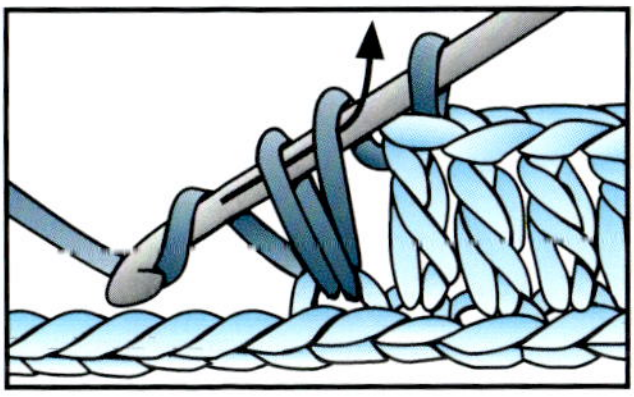

Fig. 5b

TREBLE CROCHET (abbreviated tr)

YO twice, insert hook in stitch or space indicated, YO and pull up a loop (4 loops on hook) **(Fig. 6a)**, (YO and draw through 2 loops on hook) 3 times **(Fig. 6b)**.

Fig. 6a

Fig. 6b

DOUBLE TREBLE CROCHET (abbreviated dtr)

YO 3 times, insert hook in stitch or space indicated, YO and pull up a loop (5 loops on hook) **(Fig. 7a)**, (YO and draw through 2 loops on hook) 4 times **(Fig. 7b)**.

Fig. 7a

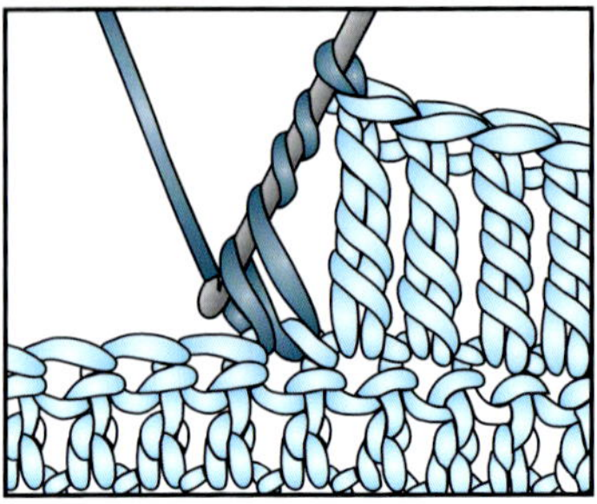

Fig. 7b

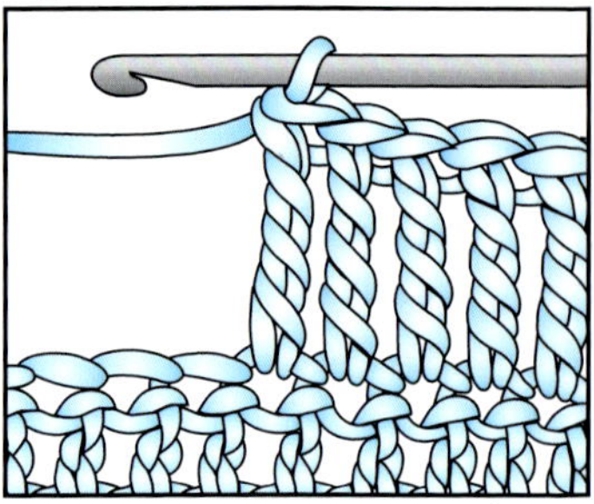

TRIPLE TREBLE CROCHET (abbreviated tr tr)

YO 4 times, insert hook in stitch or space indicated, YO and pull up a loop (6 loops on hook) **(Fig. 8a)**, (YO and draw through 2 loops on hook) 5 times **(Fig. 8b)**.

Fig. 8a

Fig. 8b

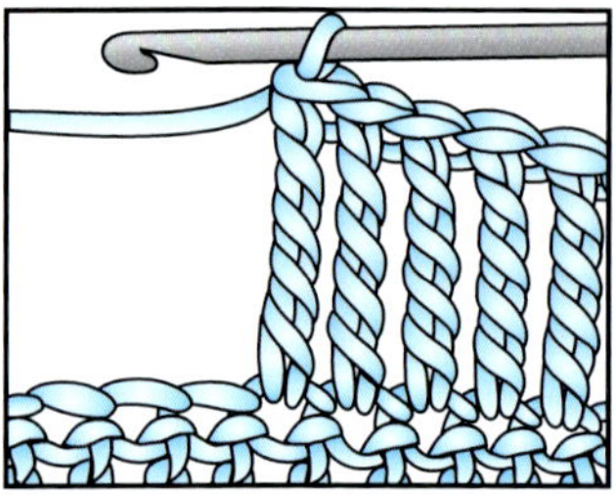

POPCORNS

A Popcorn consists of a group of stitches, usually four or five dc, worked in one stitch or space and drawn together at the top **(Fig. 9a)**.

For example, work 5 dc in next dc, drop loop from hook, insert hook in first dc of 5-dc group, hook dropped loop and draw through to form Popcorn **(Fig. 9b)**.

Fig. 9a **4-dc**

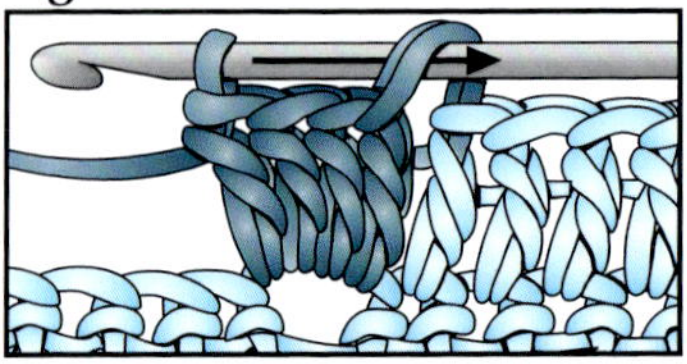

Fig. 9b **5-dc**

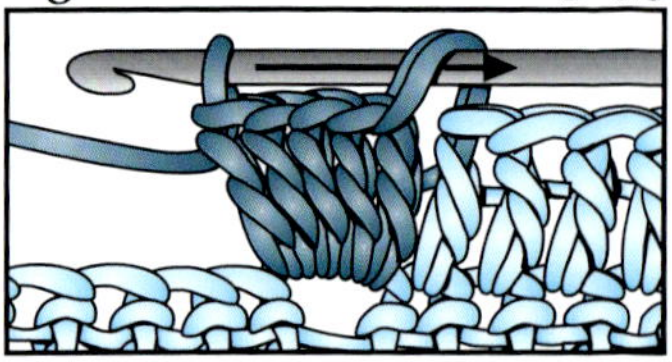

CLUSTERS

A Cluster is any combination of stitches each worked to the last step and joined together at the top. Clusters can be worked all in the same stitch or space **(Figs. 10a & b) or** across several stitches or spaces **(Figs. 11a & b)**.
For example, ★ YO, insert hook in stitch indicated, YO and pull up a loop, YO and draw through 2 loops on hook; repeat from ★ 2 times **more**, YO and draw through all 4 loops on hook **(Fig. 10a)**.

Fig. 10a

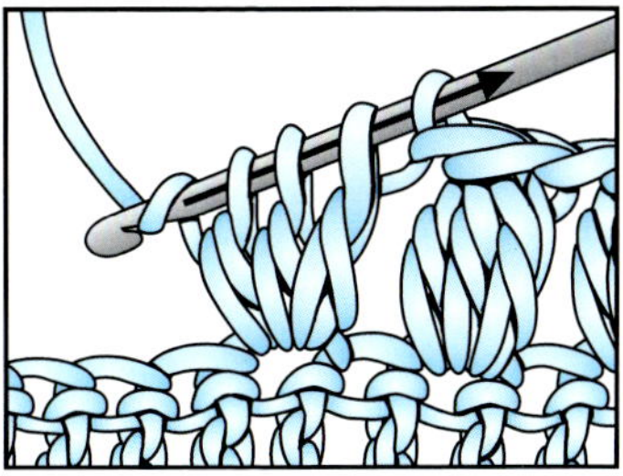

Fig. 10b

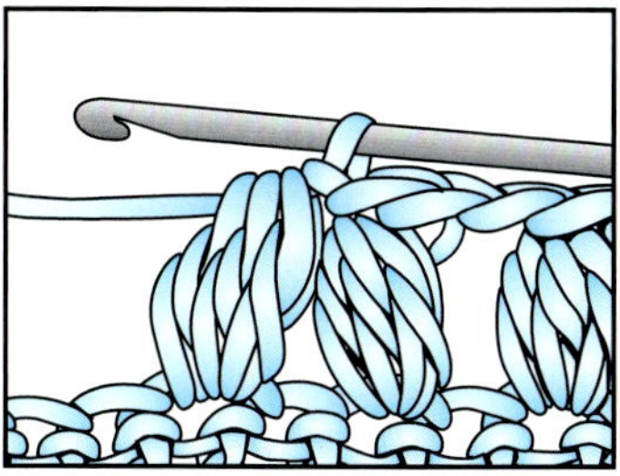

Fig. 11a

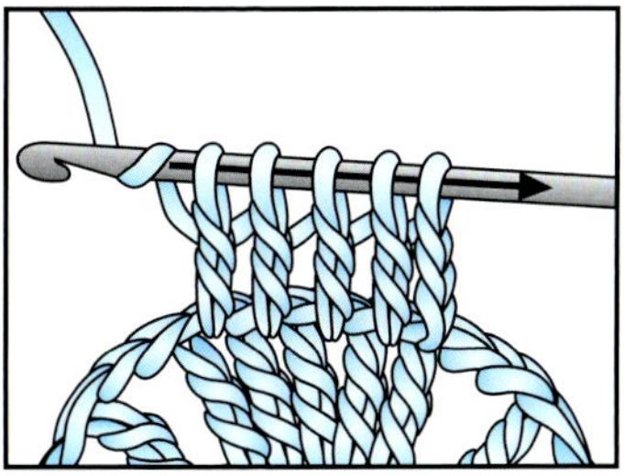

Fig. 11b

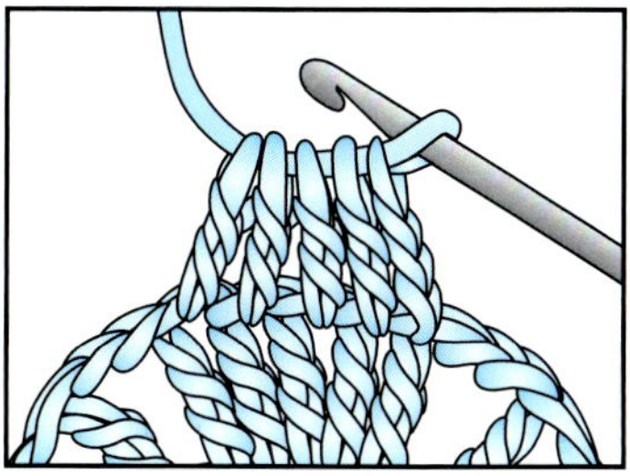

PUFF STITCHES

A Puff stitch consists of loops joined together at the top.
For example, ★ YO, insert hook in stitch or space indicated, YO and pull up a loop **even** with loop on hook; repeat from ★ 2 times **more**, YO and draw through all 7 loops on hook **(Fig. 12)**.

Fig. 12

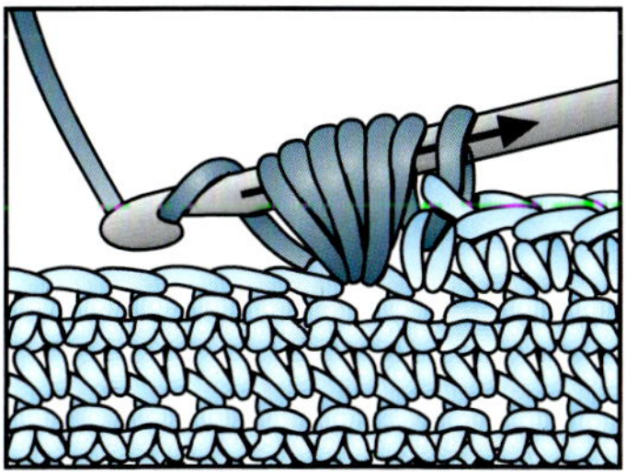

SHELLS

A Shell is any combination of dc or tr worked into one stitch or space and separated by one or more chains, **or** a group of dc or tr worked into one stitch or space.

For example, work (2 dc, ch 1, 2 dc) in next ch-1 space **(Fig. 13a)**, **or** work 5 dc in center dc of next Shell **(Fig. 13b)**.

Fig. 13a

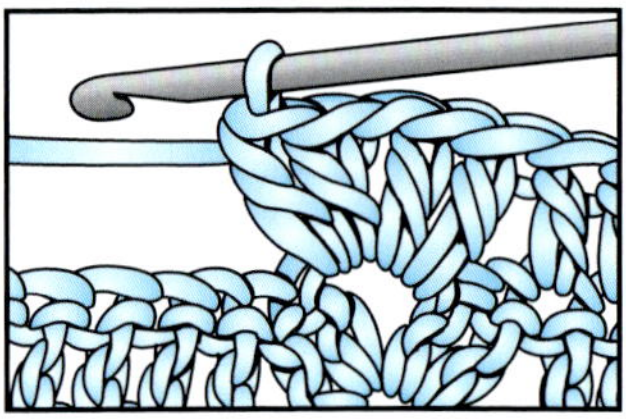

Fig. 13b

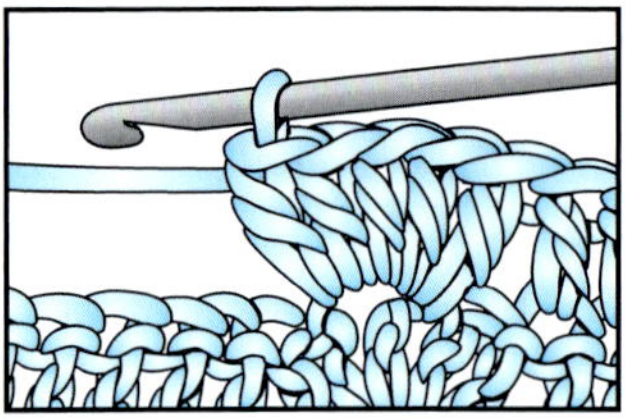

V-STITCHES

A V-Stitch consists of 2 dc or tr worked into one stitch or space and separated by chains.

For example, skip next dc, work (dc, ch 3, dc) in next dc **(Fig. 14)**.

Fig. 14

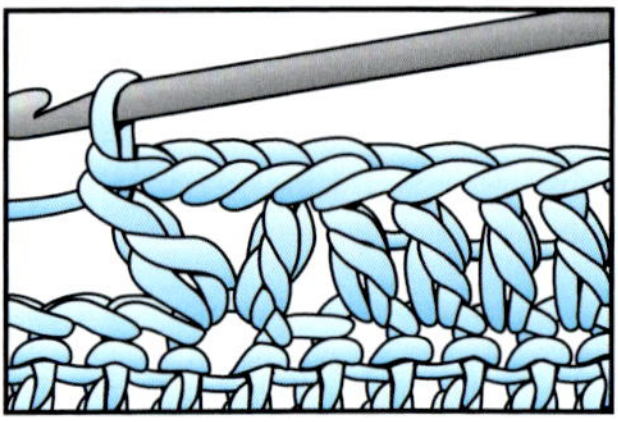

GAUGE

Exact gauge is **essential** for proper size. Before beginning your project, make a sample swatch in the yarn or thread and hook specified. After completing the swatch, measure it with the ruler given, counting your stitches and rows or rounds carefully. If your swatch is larger or smaller than specified, **make another, changing hook size to get the correct gauge**. Keep trying until you find the size hook that will give you the specified gauge.

CROSS STITCHES

A Cross Stitch is formed when a dc or tr "crosses" a stitch previously made, working into a skipped stitch. It can be worked **around**, in **front** of, or **behind** the stitch just made **(Fig. 28)**.

For example, skip next dc, dc in next dc, dc in skipped dc working **around** dc just made **(Figs. 15a & b)**.

Fig. 15a

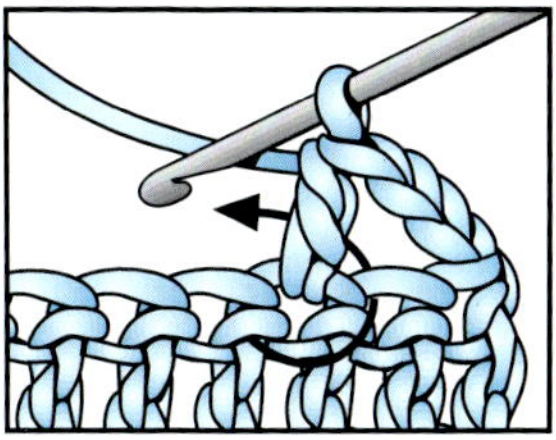

Fig. 15b

LONG STITCHES

Long stitches are usually worked **around** one or more rows or rounds **(Fig. 28)**, **or around** a group of stitches. Work sc, hdc, or dc, inserting hook in stitch or space indicated, and pulling up a loop **even** with loop on hook; complete stitch **(Fig. 16)**.

Fig. 16

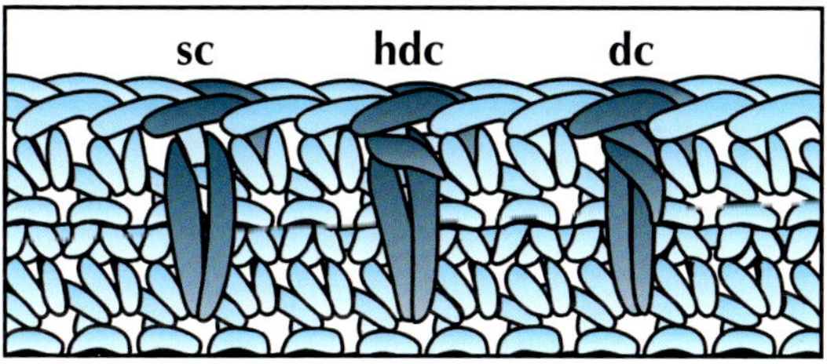

CABLE

Sc in next sc, ★ ch 3 **loosely**, skip next 2 sc, sc in next sc, **turn**; sc in next 3 chs **(Fig. 17a)**, slip stitch in next sc (sc made before ch-3) **(Fig. 17b)**, **turn**; working **behind** Cable, sc in 2 skipped sc **(Fig. 17c)**; repeat from ★ across.

Fig. 17a

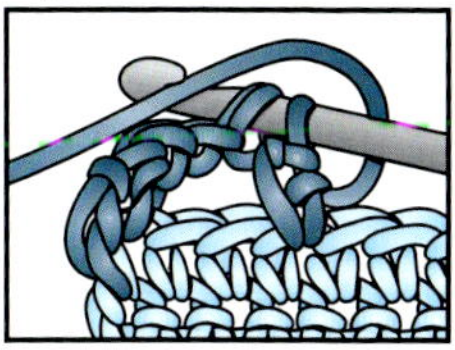

Fig. 17b

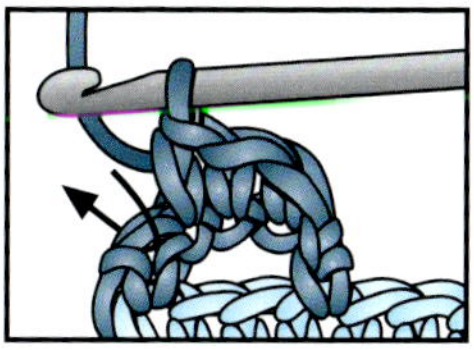

Fig. 17c

POST STITCHES

Work any stitch around post of stitch indicated, inserting hook in direction of arrow **(Fig. 18)**.

Fig. 18

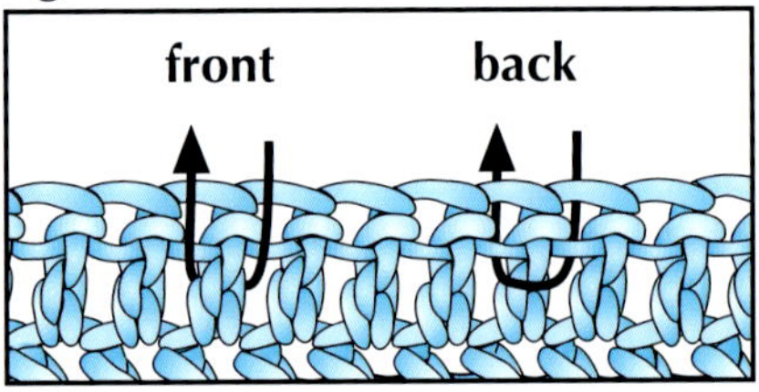

FRONT POST DOUBLE CROCHET

(abbreviated FPdc)

YO, insert hook from **front** to **back** around post of stitch indicated **(Fig. 18)**, YO and pull up a loop (3 loops on hook) **(Fig. 19)**, (YO and draw through 2 loops on hook) twice.

Fig. 19

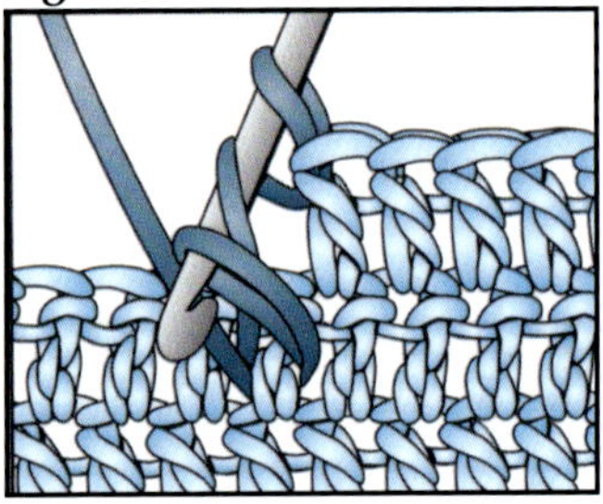

BACK POST DOUBLE CROCHET

(abbreviated BPdc)

YO, insert hook from **back** to **front** around post of stitch indicated **(Fig. 18)**, YO and pull up a loop (3 loops on hook) **(Fig. 20)**, (YO and draw through 2 loops on hook) twice.

Fig. 20

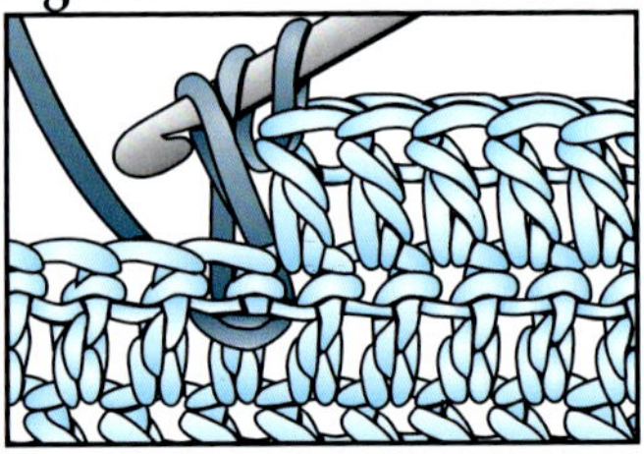

REVERSE SINGLE CROCHET
(abbreviated reverse sc)

Working from **left** to **right**, insert hook in stitch to right of hook **(Fig. 21a)**, YO and draw through, under and to left of loop on hook **(Fig. 21b)**, YO and draw through both loops on hook **(Figs. 21c & d)**.

Fig. 21a

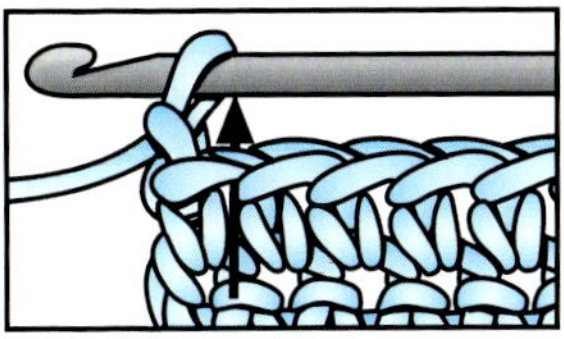

Fig. 21b

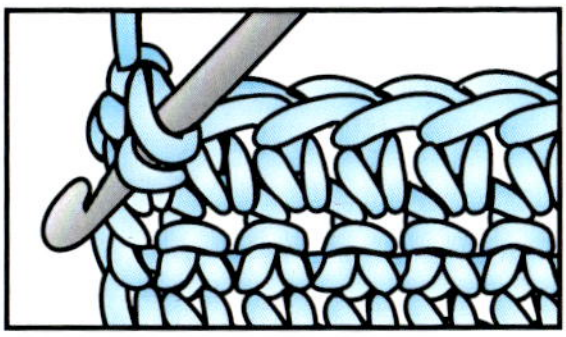

Fig. 21c

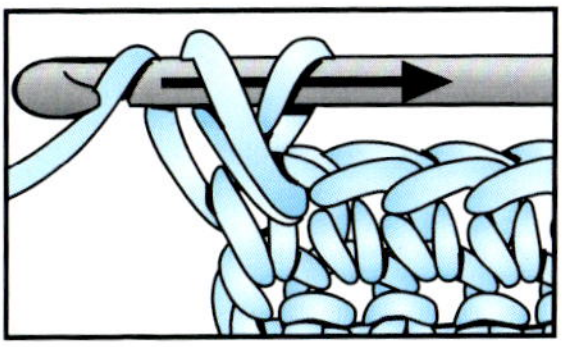

Fig. 21d

REVERSE HALF DOUBLE CROCHET
(abbreviated reverse hdc)

Working from **left** to **right**, YO, insert hook in stitch to right of hook **(Fig. 22a)**, YO and draw through, under and to left of loop on hook **(Fig. 22b)**, YO and draw through all 3 loops on hook **(Figs. 22c & d)**.

Fig. 22a

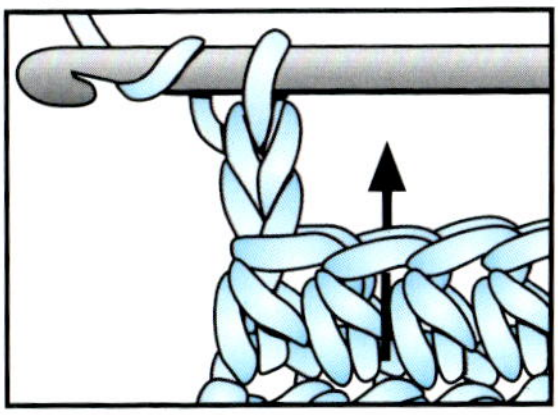

Fig. 22b

Fig. 22c

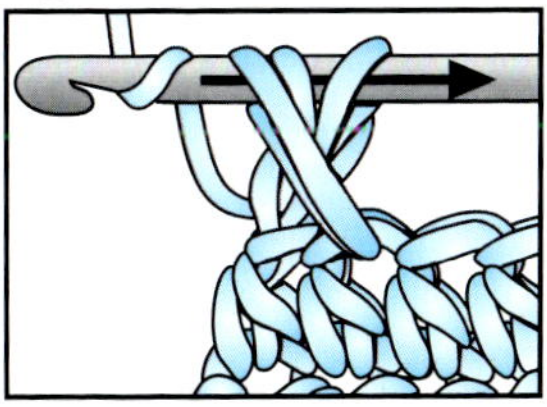

Fig. 22d

JOINING WITH SLIP STITCH

Begin with a slip knot on hook. Insert hook in stitch or space indicated, YO and draw through the stitch or space **and** the loop on hook.

JOINING WITH SC

Begin with a slip knot on hook. Insert hook in stitch or space indicated, YO and pull up a loop, YO **(Fig. 23a)** and draw through both loops on hook **(Fig. 23b)**.

Fig. 23a

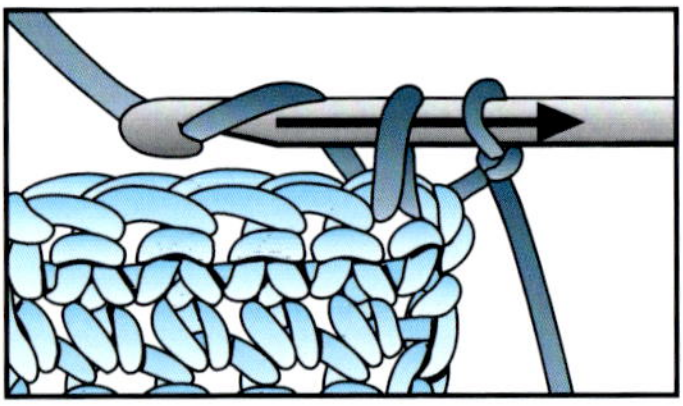

Fig. 23b

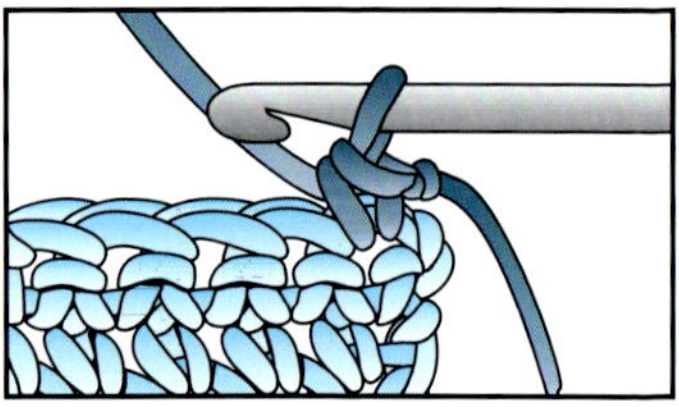

JOINING WITH HDC

Begin with a slip knot on hook. YO, holding loop on hook, insert hook in stitch or space indicated, YO and pull up a loop, YO and draw through all 3 loops on hook.

JOINING WITH DC

Begin with a slip knot on hook. YO, holding loop on hook, insert hook in stitch or space indicated, YO and pull up a loop (3 loops on hook), (YO and draw through 2 loops on hook) twice.

BACK OR FRONT LOOP ONLY

Always work under both top loops, unless specified to work in Back or Front Loops Only as indicated by arrow **(Fig. 24)**.

Fig. 24

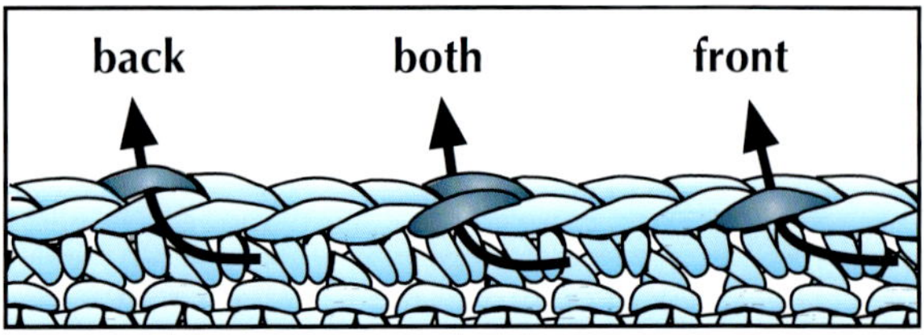

FREE LOOPS

After working in Back or Front Loops Only on a row or round, there will be a ridge of unused loops. These are called the free loops. Later, when instructed to work in the free loops of the same row or round, work in these loops **(Fig. 25a)**.

When instructed to work in the free loops of a chain, work in loop indicated by arrow **(Fig. 25b)**.

Fig. 25a

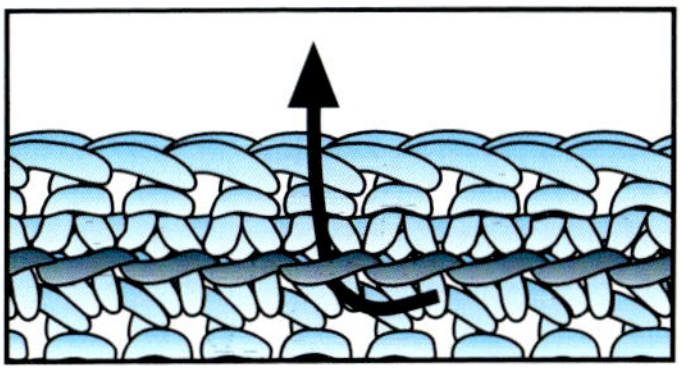

Fig. 25b

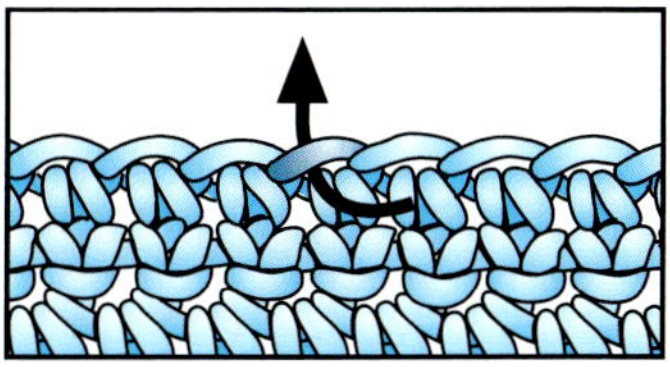

WORKING BETWEEN OR BEFORE STITCHES

When instructed to work in spaces **between** stitches or in space **before** a stitch, insert hook in space indicated by arrow **(Fig. 26)**.

Fig. 26

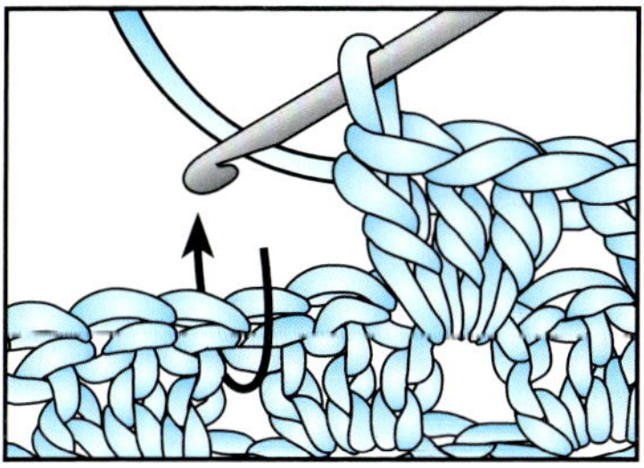

WORKING IN TOP OF A STITCH

When working in top of a stitch **just worked**, insert hook as indicated by arrow **(Fig. 27)**.

Fig. 27

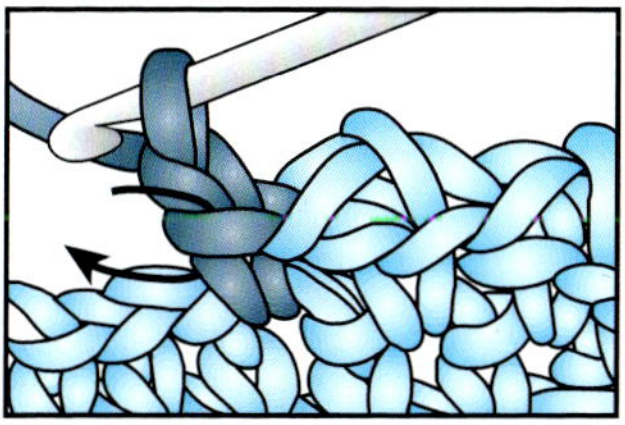

WORKING IN FRONT OF, AROUND, OR BEHIND A STITCH

Work in stitch or space indicated, inserting hook as indicated by arrow **(Fig. 28)**.

Fig. 28

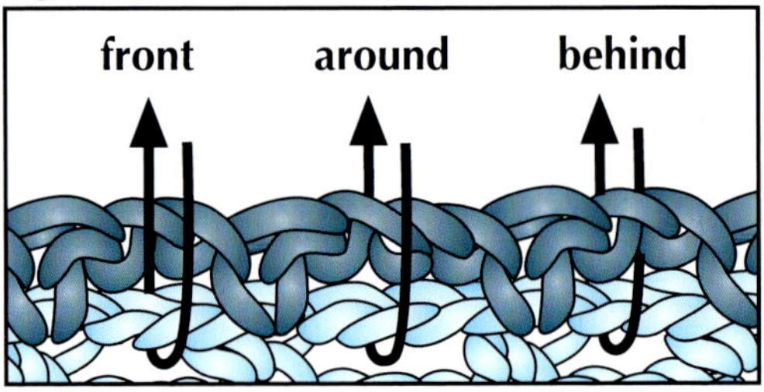

CHANGING COLORS

Work the last stitch to within one step of completion, drop old yarn, hook new yarn **(Fig. 29a)** and draw through all loops on hook. Cut old yarn and work over both ends unless otherwise instructed.

When working in rounds, drop old yarn and join with slip stitch to first stitch using new yarn **(Fig. 29b)**.

Fig. 29a

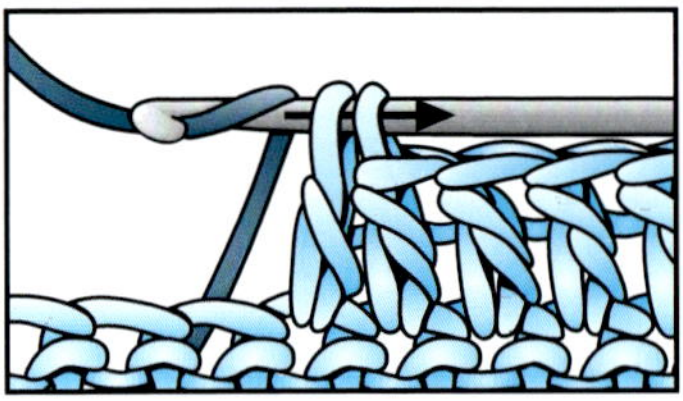

Fig. 29b

NO-SEW JOINING

Squares, Motifs, and Strips can be joined together as the last round is worked. Holding pieces with **wrong** sides together, work slip stitch or sc in corresponding space on previous piece **(Fig. 30)**.

Fig. 30

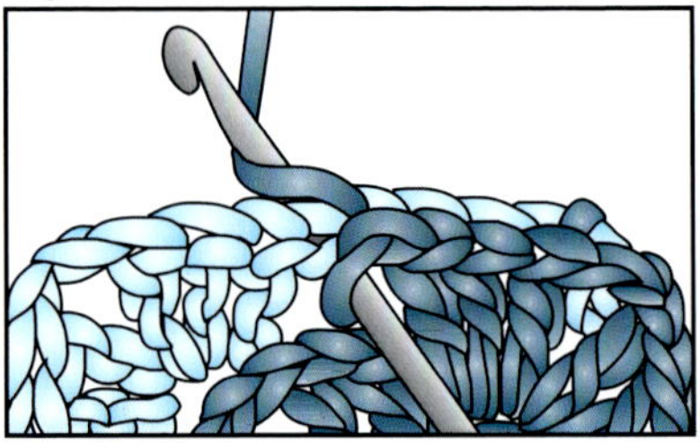